Old MAUCHLINE and TARBO

with CROSSHANDS, FAILFORD and STA

by
John Hood

When Mauchline's New Road was formed, it was found necessary to demolish some of the houses on the north side of the Cross. These houses ran in a continuous line from the corner of High Street (beside the horse and cart in the photograph) to Back Causeway. Among the properties demolished was the home of James Smith, a friend of Robert Burns and brother of Jean Smith. Jean was one of the six 'Mauchline Belles' praised for their beauty in Burns's poem *The Belles of Mauchline*. The substantial building to right of picture is The Place, also known as Mauchline House or McShane's Building. Built by the Earls of Eglinton in 1756, over time it had many uses including a grocery shop and a fish shop. Although initially much admired, by the 1930s The Place had become something of an eyesore and was accordingly demolished. The Temperance Hall on the north side of New Road was also a casualty. In its time it was well used, having for a period a public library located in its lesser hall.

First published in the United Kingdom, 2001,
by Stenlake Publishing,
Telephone / Fax: 01290 551122

ISBN 1 84033 172 0

THE PUBLISHERS REGRET THAT THEY CANNOT SUPPLY
COPIES OF ANY PICTURES FEATURED IN THIS BOOK.

ACKNOWLEDGEMENTS

I would like to thank the following people for their help in compiling this book: Derek Barber, Failford; Tom Barclay, Local History Librarian, Carnegie Library, Ayr; Hugh Candlish, Failford; Enoch Currie, Curator, Bachelors' Club, Tarbolton; Anne Geddes, Community Librarian (Heritage Services), Cumnock; Shirley Gillespie, Tarbolton Library; George Hardy, Mauchline; Terry Harrison, Mauchline; Liz Jackson, Tarbolton; Jan Kelso, Curator, Burns House Museum, Mauchline; and Donald Nelson, Mitchell Library, Glasgow. The publishers wish to thank William Irwin for permission to reproduce the photograph on page 6.

FURTHER READING

The books listed below were used by the author during his research. None of them are available from Stenlake Publishing. Those interested in finding out more are advised to contact their local bookshop or reference library.

A.M. Boyle, *The Ayrshire Book of Burns-lore*, 1985.
East Ayrshire Council Library Service, *Mauchline Past and Present*, 1996.
J.T. Gibb, *The Land of Burns, Mauchline, Town and District*, 1911.
T. Killen, *Guide to Mauchline, Catrine, Sorn and surrounding district*, 1909.
E.H. Letham, *Burns and Tarbolton*, 1900.
D.I. Lyell (ed.), *Mauchline in Times Past*, 1986.
J. Strawthorn and W. Boyd, *The Third Statistical Account of Scotland: Ayrshire*, 1951.

Among the tombstones in Tarbolton churchyard is one erected in memory of a local farmer, John Lambie, who died on 17 August 1863. In addition to his farm, Lambie owned land and property on Hood's Hill. His grandson (seen here in this 1890s photograph with Mauchline carpenter Matthew Hamilton, an old school friend) claimed that Lambie was a contemporary of Robert Burns. The farmer John Lambie is not, however, to be confused with the gaudsboy with the same name who was employed at Mossgiel by Burns and who claimed to have been leading the plough when the poet disturbed the mouse's nest which led him to pen *To a Mouse*.

INTRODUCTION

Although the district around Mauchline and Tarbolton is deservedly known the world over for its associations with Scotland's national poet, Robert Burns, it would be wrong to imagine that there is little else to the history of the district.

In AD 681 a tribe called the Cruithni (possibly of Pictish origin) were defeated on Mauchline Moor by the people of Strathclyde. Later, in 1165, Walter the High Steward of Scotland gave land in Mauchline, Sorn and Muirkirk parishes (cumulatively known as Kylemuir) to the Cistercian Abbey of Melrose. The tower known as Mauchline Castle was built by the Abbey around 1450 and was used by the monks for administrative purposes. In 1510 Mauchline was made into a Burgh of Barony. Later, the remainder of the Abbey lands were handed over to the powerful Loudoun family and, ultimately, fell into the hands of other wealthy and powerful families, such as the Campbells, Cunninghames, Montgomeries and Reids. In 1671 neighbouring Tarbolton was also made into a Burgh of Barony, but unlike Mauchline, retains its status to this day. In the seventeenth century, the district (like much of the south-west of Scotland) suffered badly for its Covenanting beliefs, especially during the period known as the 'Killing Times'. Adherents to the National Covenant, who resisted new Anglican forms of worship, were gradually hunted down and persecuted. In 1648, for example, a troop of mounted dragoons routed Covenanter rebels on the moors outside Mauchline, and in 1685 five captured Covenanters were summarily tried and hanged on Mauchline's Loan Green. Tarbolton likewise suffered for its Covenanting beliefs. The famous Covenanter minister, Alexander Peden (at one time a minister in Tarbolton), spent five years of his life imprisoned on the Bass Rock, before escaping. He remained in hiding until his death from natural causes in 1686.

Although coal was mined and stone quarried from early times, the district was, until the beginning of the seventeenth century, predominantly a farming community. After that time, colonies of handloom weavers settled in the area (most notably in Tarbolton) and found employment producing firstly linen, but later cotton and silk, goods. Initially this work was done in the weavers' houses, but as the century progressed numerous water-powered lint mills and cotton works were erected on the banks of the River Ayr and its tributaries. At the Haugh, for example, there was a lint mill and, later, a woollen mill. There was also an ice stone (or curling stone) factory. The nearby 'model village' of Catrine owed its existence to the large cotton works established in 1787 by Claud Alexander of Ballochmyle, in association with the philanthropist, David Dale.

Coal mining, which was carried out on a small scale at Fail in the fifteenth century, dramatically increased in the nineteenth century to become another important local industry. At its peak, coal production in Ayrshire was surpassed in size only by neighbouring Lanarkshire. The commercial extraction of coal from the Enterkine pits at Annbank, and other local pits including Mauchline and Lochlea, hastened the development of the Glasgow & South Western Railway Company's network of lines from the mid-1800s onwards. By the early 1900s the local communities were largely dependent on the prosperity of the mining industry, although others found employment in, for example, the production of powdered milk products and margarine, and the manufacture of curling stones, spectacle frames and Mauchline Ware. The latter two industries were centred around Mauchline and for much of the early 1900s were major employers of local people.

In that period the mining industry prospered, with over three million tons of coal brought to the surface in 1948. However, after the nationalisation of the industry, the National Coal Board embarked on a rationalisation exercise which saw many of the local collieries closed down in favour of a few larger and more modern pits. By 1950 there were still 11,500 miners employed in the Ayrshire pits, but gradually local miners were being bussed as far afield as Prestwick. In 1989 the last Ayrshire pit was closed. A similar industry, the quarrying of new red sandstone, which had been carried out since the eighteenth century, was also in decline as cheaper brick supplanted the more durable, but more expensive, sandstone. At its peak several hundred men were employed in the local quarries, but by 1951 only Ballochmyle Quarry was still in operation.

Inevitably, however, it was the Burns connection that brought (and still brings) visitors into the area from all parts of the world. In days gone by interest in Burns was long-satisfied by the regular tours of the 'Land of Burns' which visited the many places associated with the poet. Nowadays it is still possible to see (albeit much changed in appearance) farms such as Lochlea and Mossgiel where the Burns family lived and worked, and Willie's Mill in Tarbolton where the poet's wife, Jean Armour, temporarily lodged. Properties like the world famous Bachelors' Club at Tarbolton, where the poet and like-minded friends met to debate, and Poosie Nansie's Inn at Mauchline continue to attract visitors, although the more romantically inclined may choose instead to visit nearby Failford where it has long been said Burns parted from Highland Mary. Whatever their inclination, however, the ultimate place of pilgrimage for Burns lovers has for many years been the historic churchyard at Mauchline where the poet's children and many of his contemporaries are buried.

Within the last fifty years, in addition to the demise of mining and quarrying, other local industries such as snuff box and curling stone manufacture have largely disappeared. Today, however, along with farming, tourism is one of the mainstays of the local economy.

The hamlet of Crosshands stands at the junction of the Kilmarnock–Dumfries and Galston–Tarbolton roads, approximately two miles north-west of Mauchline. Little has changed since this photograph was taken. The whitewashed building, Crosshands House, has several stables to its rear which suggest that at one time it may have been a coaching inn. In fact, the adjacent property is called Stables Cottage. Woodholm, the two-storey building to the right of picture, was built in 1848. Although now a private dwelling house, it served as the local school until the 1940s. Today, local children attend the more modern Crossroads Primary School. Also in the picture is the private house, Taliskar.

At one time there were several local sawmills in the Mauchline area, supplying wood for local industries such as the box works factories, which produced the decorative snuff boxes known as Mauchline Ware. The sawmill in the photograph was at Crosshands. Apparently, during the First World War, Canadian soldiers (many of whom had been lumberjacks in civilian life) worked in the sawmill.

The Mauchline Dykefield Colliery on the northern outskirts of Mauchline was opened in 1938 and provided much needed employment for the village and surrounding area. In 1951, for example, it was employing 800 miners, most of whom were brought in by bus from communities such as Dreghorn, Crosshouse, Kilmarnock, Hurlford and Galston. At that time it was producing a quarter of a million tons of coal a year. By the 1960s the colliery was operated by the National Coal Board which was rationalising the industry, causing massive redundancies in the industry nationwide. Smaller pits were closed down and production concentrated on fewer, larger, pits. On Friday, 26 August 1966, it was the turn of the Mauchline pit. It closed, with the transfer of 250 miners to the new Barony Colliery at nearby Auchinleck.

A little beyond Willie's Mill the B744 rises sharply as it enters Tarbolton at the Moat. In earlier times a motte and bailey castle stood on the summit of the hill. It was here that justice would have been dispensed by the feudal lord, with executions being carried out at nearby Gallows Hill. Until 1927 Moat Hill was also where the annual June bonfires were lit – a relic of pre-Christian rituals. Traditionally, on these occasions, the children would go round each house collecting fuel for the bonfire. At one time the Moat was commonly referred to as Hood's Hill, in memory of a local schoolmaster who allowed his pupils to use the hill as a playground. From the brow of the Moat there are excellent views of Burns Street with its nineteenth century Town House, and, beyond, Tarbolton Parish Church on Cunningham Street.

Burns Street (once known as Baker's Brae) runs from Tarbolton Cross to Garden Street and is much changed from when this photograph was taken. The Burns Tavern and adjacent properties to the left of picture are now gone. The row of single-storey thatched roof cottages still remain, although they now have slated roofs. The historic properties of Tibbie Stein's House and Manson's Inn at one time stood on the opposite corners of where Burns Street and Garden Street meet. On Garden Street itself, and facing on to Burns Street, is 'Brainch', formerly an inn, but now a private house. To the right of the picture is the Town House which dates from 1832. This served as the meeting place for the bailies and councillors elected by the villagers of Tarbolton, a right given to them when the village was granted Free Burgh of Barony status during the reign of Charles II. The Town House is partially disused at present, a car repair business currently occupying part of the property.

The Cross, Tarbolton.

The properties to the left of this picture on Montgomerie Street (including the long-established Tarbolton Pharmacy, post office and Plough Inn) remain largely intact. The Bachelors' Club also remains, although other properties at the Cross have not been so fortunate. The Co-operative Society store and Dr Patrick Wodrow's manse in Sandgate, for example, are both gone. Also changed is the corner site at Montgomerie Street and Cunningham Street. Long occupied by Jean Logan's grocery shop, this area is now landscaped. During Burns's time the site was occupied by the Cross Keys Inn and it was here, on 8 July 1782, that the Lodge St James was re-formed. At one point Burns served as Depute Master of the lodge and on 9 August 1844 three of Burns's sons were made honorary members.

In June 1781 two local Masonic lodges, St David and St James, amalgamated to form a single lodge. A little over a week later, in Manson's Inn, Robert Burns was made a freemason of this newly-formed lodge. The inn, a single-storey thatched roof property, was at that time run by a James Manson. Although the inn is no longer standing, a metal plaque marks its location. The amalgamated lodge had barely lasted a year when Lodge St James broke away and reformed, with James Manson as treasurer. Lodge St David continued in Tarbolton until 1843.

Burns' Bachelors' Club, Tarbolton.

The most prominent building in Sandgate is the historic Bachelors' Club, the last remaining pre-eighteenth century two-storey property in Tarbolton. During Burns's lifetime it was an inn run by John Richard, the ground floor being used as living quarters and the upper floor (which was accessed by an outside staircase) for dances. Burns, his brother Gilbert, and some friends formed a debating society here on 11 November 1780. It would appear that John Richard was quite enterprising, for he not only sold spirits, but brewed his own ale and made his own wooden barrels. Over the years the property has been used for living accommodation, and also as a brewery and a byre. At one time it was requisitioned by the army. By the 1930s the building was in a state of disrepair and in 1937 was threatened with demolition. However, due to the efforts of local bodies and the National Trust for Scotland, it was saved and restored. Because of wartime restrictions, it wasn't until October 1951 that James C. Stormonth Darling, Secretary of the National Trust for Scotland, declared the Bachelors' Club reopened.

Back Street Tarbolton

Although the area to the right is now occupied by council housing, the row of single-storey cottages opposite remain largely unchanged, as does 'The Cottage' in the far distance. Perhaps the cottages were once occupied by the many weavers and miners who worked in Tarbolton. At one time Tarbolton had a thriving muslin weaving industry with 120 looms in operation. Later, the weaving of silk was introduced into the village. In fact, a local girl was selected to demonstrate this skill to Queen Victoria at the Glasgow Exhibition in 1851. From a peak of 280 weavers, the industry gradually declined until, in 1920, the last silk weaver, Robert Wilson, retired. Tarbolton was eventually also a mining village. Reputedly the first miner to settle in what was then a predominantly weaving community was 'stoned' by the villagers. Notwithstanding this, more miners settled in the area and miner's rows were built to accommodate them. Many of the miners worked at local pits such as Annbank and Drongan, although latterly many of them were transported to Prestwick after all the smaller pits closed down.

In this early view of Cunningham Street the corner sites are occupied by the old Cross Keys Inn (left) and the Burns Tavern (right), both now gone. The former was bought by a local man, James Brown, who for a period had been an overseer on his uncle's sugar plantation in Virginia, USA. He converted the property into a house and licensed grocers, and renamed it 'Virginia'. The Burns Tavern (also known as Murchie's Tavern) stood at the corner of Burns Street. Interestingly, this street neither takes its name from the tavern or any association with Robert Burns, but apparently from the fact that the Fail, or Bennal's, Burn (which rises on higher ground near Failford and empties into Fail Loch) flows under it.

The character of Dr Hornbrook in *Death and Doctor Hornbrook* was modelled on John Wilson, a schoolmaster at Tarbolton from 1781 to 1790. Wilson had earlier taught at Craigie, near Lochlea Farm, and had been secretary of Lodge St James, Tarbolton, and was therefore known to Burns. According to some, Wilson left Tarbolton because he was unhappy with the way he was depicted in the poem; however, others maintain that he remained on friendly terms with the poet, indeed he apparently later sought a character reference from him! While at Tarbolton, Wilson stayed in Cunningham Street in the two-storied thatched house beyond the tavern. He taught in the local school which was situated a little further along, on the opposite side of the street beside Tarbolton Parish Church. The house was renovated and reduced to a single-storey property around 1911. John Wilson ultimately settled in Glasgow and is buried in Gorbals Cemetery.

Tarbolton Parish Church in Cunningham Street was built in 1821. Designed by architect Robert Johnson, it is square in appearance, with a projecting frontage topped by a ninety foot high steeple. It stands on the site of an earlier parish church. One of its ministers, the Rev. Dr Patrick Wodrow, is mentioned in Burns's poem *The Twa Herds*. His assistant, the Rev. John McMath, was also the subject of Burns's *To the Rev. John McMath* which was written as a result of McMath's support for Burns's friend Gavin Hamilton in his dispute with Mauchline Kirk Session. In 1943 the parish church merged with the Erskine Church.

Montgomerie Street is named after the Montgomerie family, whose lineage included the Earls of Eglinton, and is Tarbolton's main street. In the 1700s single-storey thatched weavers' cottages predominated. However, in 1906 (a few years after this photograph was taken) it was described as a 'long and miserable main street'. Among the several historic buildings on Montgomerie Street today is Lodge St James Tarbolton Kilwinning No. 135, opposite the Tarbolton Gospel Hall. Initially, the lodge had met within the Cross Keys Inn, but on 12 October 1889 the foundation stone was laid for a purpose-built hall, with the first meeting being held on 2 August 1890. In 1925 a temple was added and the hall renovated through the generosity of an expatriate, Andrew Bryson, who had become a Massachusetts merchant.

The southern approach to Tarbolton, along with nearby Montgomerie Square, has been largely redeveloped. A garage now stands on the site of the property to left of picture. One of the few surviving buildings is the white harled building in the centre of the picture. This is the long-established Black Bull Inn which was well situated on the road to Tarbolton Station. It was to here that guests repaired for a meal after the official opening of the Lorimer Institute. Just out of picture, the nearby war memorial was unveiled in November 1920. Unusually, the memorial was unveiled by a civilian, James Brown MP. Headed by the Ayr Burgh Band, a parade marched from the parish church to the tune of the 'Dead March'.

The Library, Tarbolton

The Lorimer Institute in Montgomerie Street was opened in 1878. Its construction was funded by John Lorimer, a native of Tarbolton who had businesses in Glasgow and Kilmarnock. When opened, the institute comprised a library, reading and recreation rooms, and a caretaker's room. In addition the funding provided for a librarian's salary, annual additions to the library bookstock, and the purchase of a selection of newspapers and periodicals. The institute, which is built of red sandstone, was designed by Kilmarnock architect, G. Andrew.

Thomas Steen was a spirit merchant in Stair around 1930 and was proprietor of the historic Stair Inn, the hamlet's only public house. This inn (once known locally as the Bridgend Inn) dates from the 1820s and stands in close proximity to Stair Bridge. In the eighteenth century it was normal practice for worshippers to frequent the local inns after church services. The Rev. Alex Small of Stair must surely have approved of this practice since, during inclement weather, he would conduct some of his Sunday evening services within the Stair Inn and end by treating the congregation to a few glasses of ale and, occasionally, hot bowls of soup!

This uniformed gentleman may have been a railway employee or, perhaps, a postman. Until its closure in 1943, Tarbolton Station was a recognised meeting place for the local postmen waiting for the trains from Glasgow bringing their mail. During the First World War, the Tarbolton postman would typically start the day by walking the two miles to the station to meet the early morning train. After collecting his mail, he would have to sort it himself before undertaking the four-and-a-half hour trek around the district.

FAILFORD VILLAGE NEAR MAUCHLINE

The village of Failford lies on the A758, between Tarbolton and Mauchline. One of Failford's claims to fame is that it is said a tumulus (or grave) discovered in 1837 in nearby Coilsfield Park is the last resting place of Auld King Coil (better known to generations of children as Old King Cole). Coil was not in fact merely a character in a nursery rhyme, but an early Pictish king. Indeed there was a King Coil's Well, which stood on higher ground near Failford Bridge. Opposite these cottages for many years stood a hone mill, which produced the whetstones used for sharpening razors. Most of the cottages (and the long-established Failford Inn) remain today.

With the exception of the Failford Café (now gone), little has changed from this earlier view of Failford. Beyond Failford Bridge lies the single-storey white-washed Blackhill Cottage (Blackhill once being a local name for the village). A track beside the cottage leads to a memorial commemorating the final meeting of Robert Burns and Highland Mary. This was erected in May 1921 by the Burns Federation and Harland & Wolff Shipyard. Mary (variously described as a servant and nursery maid) was said to have worked for Gavin Hamilton and also at nearby Coilsfield House. In 1786, after James Armour tore up the marriage contract between Burns and his daughter Jean (thereby effectively forbidding her to marry him), Burns began courting Mary Campbell. According to folklore, Burns and Mary pledged their troth on 14 May 1786 by exchanging bibles across a running stream where the Water of Fail joins the River Ayr. It seems to have been the intention of the couple to emigrate to the West Indies, but shortly thereafter Mary died of a fever at Greenock (perhaps when making travel plans).

The Failford Café was built in the early 1920s to cater for the many tourists coming to Failford to see the reputed final meeting place of Burns and Highland Mary. The Café itself was a wooden building which, in addition to providing meals, sold petrol. The smaller hall to the rear was a later addition and was well-patronised by villagers playing summer ice and carpet bowls. It was also used for dances and, during the Second World War, was a popular venue for American service personnel based at Prestwick. The Café was demolished in 1982. The house (Mayfield), on higher ground to the left of the picture, was built in 1922.

These cottages at Failford (known locally as the almshouses) were situated alongside Imrie's sawmill, on the opposite bank of the Water of Fail from the Highland Mary memorial. They were built in 1849 with money bequeathed by a local landowner, Alexander Cooper of Failford House. In his bequest, Cooper specified that the money should be put into a trust fund and used to provide accommodation at Failford for an equal number of residents from Mauchline and Tarbolton parishes who had suffered misfortune or ill-health but had 'refrained from public begging'. In addition, they had to be over forty years of age, of good character and have been resident in either parish for at least five years. The cottages stood for over a hundred years, but in November 1943 they were ruined when fire swept through them, killing one elderly resident. Initially it was intended that they be rebuilt, although this did not happen. In the latter half of the twentieth century, with monies in the Cooper Trust accumulating, £10,000 was presented to Strathclyde Regional Council to help with the provision of accommodation for the elderly within Tarbolton Community Centre.

In February 1895 members of the Glasgow Mauchline Society met to determine the most appropriate way of commemorating the centenary of Robert Burns's death. The outcome was a decision to build the National Burns Memorial and Cottage Homes at the junction of the Kilmarnock and Tarbolton (or Skeoch) Roads. The sixty-seven foot high memorial was built in Scots Baronial style using local Ballochmyle red sandstone. It was designed by Glasgow architect William Fraser and cost over £1,500 to build, all of which was raised from a worldwide appeal. The memorial was opened on 7 May 1898 by J.G.A. Baird, MP. Some of the cottages can be seen in this photograph beyond the memorial. The reasoning behind the erection of cottages (which were intended to provide accommodation for the elderly and/or impoverished) was to highlight the fact that the poet had himself led an impoverished life.

The cottages alongside the National Burns Memorial were initially rent free. Six cottages (three singles and three doubles), which were first occupied in November 1897, were built with money left over from the memorial fundraising. In 1911 a further ten (four singles and six doubles) were provided from the estate of James Dick, a Glasgow merchant. At various times further cottages were built with monies gifted by individuals such as Mrs Margaret Drummond, or by institutions such as the Newcastle-upon-Tyne Burns Statue Fund. In 1938 the last cottage (No. 20) was built using monies gifted in memory of Robin and Isabella Urie.

From 1784 until 1788, Robert Burns and his brother, Gilbert, farmed at Mossgiel, and it was here that the poet composed some of his finest work, including *The Cotter's Saturday Night* and *To a Mouse*. In fact, it was said that locals would direct visitors to the specific field where Burns is alleged to have seen the 'wee sleekit, cow'rin, tim'rous beastie'! The original farmhouse, which was sub-let to them by Burns's friend and patron, Gavin Hamilton, was at that time little more than a thatched roof but-and-ben with a garret room accessed via a trap door. Since then the farmhouse has been altered on several occasions, most notably in 1858 when the height of the walls was increased by four feet. In 1870 the walls were again heightened and on this occasion the thatched roof was also slated. Mossgiel itself is now called East Mossgiel. It lies on the Tarbolton, or Skeoch, Road within sight of the National Burns Memorial and Cottage Homes. In 1996, on the bicentenary of the poet's death, an area at the entrance to the drive leading up to the farm was landscaped and a semi-circular stone wall and granite cairn constructed under the auspices of the Ayrshire Ploughing Society and the Ayrshire Association of Burns Clubs. Both the wall and the cairn incorporate plaques giving information on Burns's residence at Mossgiel and record the fact that around 10,000 spectators attended the Burns Bicentennial Horse Drawn Ploughing Competition held at Mossgiel on 3 March 1996.

Before the formation of New Road in 1820 (seen here to the left of the picture), travellers approaching Mauchline from the north left Kilmarnock Road at Netherplace Lodge and passed Netherplace House before entering the Cross via Back Causeway. A portion of the old route, between the lodge and Loudoun Street, is now called Netherplace Lane. Netherplace House was built in 1620 for Mungo Campbell and remained in the family until 1954. It is said that after a disagreement with Lilias Campbell, the lady of the House, Burns composed *Another* in retaliation, referring to her as 'Queen Netherplace'. Shortly after the death of Col. Mungo Hamilton-Campbell in 1951, Netherplace House was demolished and the estate broken up.

Mauchline's old toll gates and single-storey tollhouse (the latter is to the left of the picture) are both now gone, as are most of the older properties to the right of the picture. However, many of the properties on the north side of New Road, beyond the tollhouse, have survived. One of these is T. & G. Hutchison's pet shop. This used to be the offices and showroom for William and Andrew Smith's box works. The factory itself later occupied the site on which the tollhouse stood. It was one of several local factories producing the much sought after Mauchline Ware. These highly decorative snuff boxes, designed with a hidden hinge, were originally known as Laurencekirk snuff boxes as this was where they were first made. Production of the boxes in large quantities began in Ayrshire around 1820. It was at this time that brothers William and Andrew Smith opened their Mauchline factory. Production was severely disrupted in 1933, when a fire swept through the factory, and finally ceased in 1939, shortly after the retiral of the last of the Smith family. In 1963 a modern fire station was built on the site of the factory.

Mauchline Cross (or 'Cors', as Burns called it) has undergone much change since the demolition of The Place. For many years afterwards, the vacant area was used for car parking, but in 1966 a new post office was built on the site. In the mid-1990s this was demolished and a modern complex comprising housing, a library and council offices erected. Opposite, the properties on either side of Castle Street remain largely intact. The building on the extreme right has been a shoe shop and a cycle shop and is currently a dental surgery. Among the older established businesses at the Cross were James M. Jamieson (grocers), Miss Peggy McMinn (tobacconist and confectioners) and James Lambie (tailor).

Back Causeway (now Castle Street), which is so narrow it was said that 'two wheelbarrows tremble when they meet', used to be the main entrance to Mauchline Cross from the north. Robert Burns and Jean Armour briefly occupied the upper floor of the house on the extreme left in 1788. At that time the property was owned by Archibald Meikle, known locally as 'Baldy Muckle'. In 1915 the house was acquired by the Glasgow District Burns Clubs Association who renovated the property with the help of a generous donation from Charles Rennie Cowie of Glasgow. It was opened on 28 August of that year by Mrs Cowie, the upper floor being a museum and the ground floor accommodation for elderly people. The following year, the adjacent property (formerly Dr John MacKenzie's house) became part of the museum. On 6 June 1969 the properties (both having undergone further renovation) were reopened as the Burns House Museum by Sir Claud Hagart-Alexander of Ballochmyle. The white-washed property standing opposite had previously been called the Sma Inn, but by Burns's time was Auld Nanse Tinnock's Inn and was frequented by the poet. It became part of the museum and was opened on 24 May 1924 by Mrs Cowie.

The Sorn Road was formerly the old turnpike road to Muirkirk. On the outskirts of Mauchline at Jamieson Place (to the left of the picture), a view of Mauchline Hill unfolds. Also known locally as Hilltop or Sheep Hill, this 750 foot high hill has traditionally been used for bonfires and fireworks displays such as those on the occasion of King George V's Silver Jubilee and Queen Elizabeth II's coronation. It has also long been a popular walking area for Mauchline residents. On a clear day (with the aid of binoculars) it commands one of the finest views in the west of Scotland – Ben Lomond and Ben Vorlich to the north, Arran and the Rathlin Islands of Ireland to the west, and Mochrun Hill to the south. It was said of the latter view that 'when Mochrun is clear to the top the Mauchline housewives may begin to wash their blankets'!

MAUCHLINE FROM HILL TOP

At one time the Sorn Road on the outskirts of the village also provided an excellent view of Mauchline landmarks such as the tower of the parish church and the box works chimney. Although the area has been subject to change, many of the older properties remain. On the right, behind Jamieson Place, is Mauchline Primary School. This was built in 1889 on the site of the earlier Educational Institute bequeathed by James Stewart. The school has since been renovated and extended on several occasions. In front of the school on Loan Green is the Martyrs' Stone, a red freestone obelisk erected in 1885 as a memorial to five Covenanters who were hanged and buried here on 6 May 1685. Although they were not local men, Mauchline did have many adherents to the Covenanting cause and some participated in the Battle of Mauchline Moor in 1648.

This group of buildings on Loudoun Street, from the Cross on the left to Poosie Nansie's on the right, is still standing. Although most of the older established businesses have now gone, Bingham's licensed grocers remains. Present-day Mauchline Pharmacy at the corner of Loudoun Street and Earl Grey Street was, for many years, Adam Train's shoe shop, while the tearoom and bakery at No. 13 was formerly the premises of Adam McArvail, bookseller, stationer and newsagent. The latter was one of Mauchline's longest established businesses and the sign can still be seen above the doorway of the tearoom. Alex Crawford operated a painters' business in Loudoun Street from the late 1880s until the 1920s, when it became J. Meikle & Son.

Loudoun Arms. Mauchline. Post Office.

A sign to the left of the entrance to Loudoun Arms (formerly McLelland's Inn) proclaims it to be 'the home of the famous Loudoun Spout – Ayrshire's oldest artesian well'. This well, recently restored through the efforts of the Loudoun Spout Society and Mauchline Community Council, comprises a lion's head from which water pours into a trough. The present inn dates from 1856 and since 1980 has been the home of the Mauchline Burns Club. Mclelland's Inn was frequented by Burns who attended a reading club there. Opposite the inn, at the entrance to Barskimming Road, is the property occupied then (as now) by Mauchline Post Office which opened on 23 May 1905. The upper portion of this building housed reading and recreation rooms, which included a billiard room and facilities for summer ice and carpet bowls. In 1909 the annual membership fee of the reading club amounted to two shillings and sixpence (present day 12½p), with non-members charged one penny for admission.

On Loudoun Street is Mauchline Parish Church. Opposite, at the corner of Cowgate, is Poosie Nansie's hostelry. During Burns's lifetime, the parish church minister was the renowned William 'Daddy' Auld, a devout Christian and fierce critic of the poet and his friend, Gavin Hamilton. Much of the criticism towards Burns was directed to his adulterous affair with Jean Armour, the poet having several times being summoned before the Kirk Session. Ultimately, however, Burns had his revenge by satirising Auld and his Kirk Session in poems like *Holy Willie's Prayer* and *The Holy Fair*. The church had the misfortune to be in close proximity to two of Mauchline's most frequented public houses, the aforementioned Poosie Nansie's and the Whitefoord Arms (said to be the poet's favourite 'howff'). Although the latter inn no longer stands, its location is marked by a plaque. Its owner, John Dove, was variously referred to by Burns as Johnnie Doo or Johnnie Pigeon.

Burnfoot Lodge is situated within Barskimming Estate, in close proximity to Barskimming House. The lodge, which once marked the western boundary of the estate, can be reached from either the Ayr or Barskimming Road. Both the stone bridge at the lodge and an older seventeenth century bridge situated beside it on lower ground are largely unchanged. The lodge itself, which stands on top of a red sandstone cliff, has been altered and extended over the years. At the base of the cliff is a two-roomed house which has been carved into the sandstone. This house can be accessed by means of a path to the rear of the lodge and is nowadays used as a workshop by the tenant of the lodge. The house is by no means unusual, for within the estate there are other such structures carved out of the soft sandstone.

The historic Barskimming auld bridge on the Mauchline to Stair road, with its 100 foot span over the River Ayr, was built by Sir Thomas Miller (later Lord Glenlee) in the late 1700s. The bridge is still in use today, but Bridge Cottage to right of picture is now gone. The cottage was once occupied by a Mr Kemp and his daughter Kate, whom Robert Burns was attracted to. One evening, while walking out from Mauchline in the hope of meeting Kate, he bumped into his friend, James Andrew, a miller at nearby Barskimming Mill, who was also interested in Kate. It is said that after his meeting with Andrew, the poet composed *Man was made to Mourn*. The four-storey mill (seen to the left of the picture), alongside the dam, was renovated in the 1830s. It was later replaced by a new mill which was destroyed by fire in the 1890s, but subsequently rebuilt. When William Alexander (the successor to James Andrew's grandson, who was also called James Andrew) died, the mill was sold to Charles Ross. It ceased production in the late 1960s.

Life in the 'big houses', although appearing idyllic, was often not without drama and Barskimming House (said to be one of the finest houses in Ayrshire) was no exception. In March 1882 the first Barskimming House was razed to the ground when a fire broke out in the kitchen area. At the time the house was occupied by Archibald Buchanan, a partner in nearby Catrine Cotton Mill. The fire was first discovered by servants around six o'clock in the morning when, according to newspaper accounts, the cook, on opening the pantry door, was met with a 'rush of flames and smoke'. So rapidly did the fire spread that Archibald, his wife and servants, had to flee in their nightclothes. Unfortunately, they were unable to get sufficient water from the nearby river to control the fire because of the steepness of the riverbank. By the time fire engines from Mauchline and Buchanan's own Catrine works arrived, the fire had gained too strong a hold for the house to be saved and as it had just been renovated with new furniture installed, the loss was even more grievous. One of the few family heirlooms which were saved was a portrait of Lord Glenlee by Henry Raeburn.

In 1377 King Robert II granted the estate of Barskimming to Willielmo Rede de Barskemyn. The family held the estate until 1615, when it was sold to the Stewarts. In 1691 it passed to the Miller family, one of whom, Sir Thomas Miller, built the auld bridge and the first Barskimming House, which was destroyed by fire. The present house, seen here, dates from 1883. In the first half of the last century the house passed to the Galbraith family, but in 1939 was requisitioned by the army. After the Second World War it became an approved school for boys, before being handed back to the Galbraiths in 1957. It is presently occupied by Lord Strathclyde, Leader of the House of Lords.

This historic old churchyard was where Mauchline's holy fairs were held. These fairs would usually last for a full day and local and visiting preachers would gives sermons throughout. However, many people attending the fairs viewed them as more of a social event and an opportunity to drink heavily. It was in his poem *The Holy Fair* that Burns wrote about these excesses, with particular reference to Mauchline Holy Fair. The churchyard is also the final resting place for four of Robert Burns's family and many of his friends and acquaintances. Amongst these are Gavin Hamilton, Nanse Tinnock, 'Daddy Auld' and William Fisher. Also in the picture are Gavin Hamilton's house, Mauchline Castle, the North Church and the area known as the Knowe.

Gavin Hamilton's House and Castle, Mauchline.

Mauchline Castle (also known as Abbot Hunter's Tower) was erected around 1450. It is possible that it may have been used by the monks of Melrose Abbey as at one time they owned much of the surrounding land. During the Covenanting period the castle was used to house prisoners. It is now in poor condition, having lain disused for some time. The white-washed house abutting the western gable of the castle was the home of Burns's friend, patron and landlord, Gavin Hamilton. It is said that Burns married Jean Armour in an upper room within the house. It is also claimed that Burns met Mary Campbell through Hamilton. Hamilton, who was a lawyer in Mauchline, encouraged Burns to publish his poems. They developed a close friendship and, not surprisingly, Burns rallied to Hamilton's support when he was accused of various transgressions (these included picking potatoes on the Sabbath day!). Hamilton's principal accuser was a local church elder, William Fisher, whose alleged hypocrisy Burns mocked (in retaliation) in *Holy Willie's Prayer*.

In the eighteenth century the principal entrance to Mauchline from the south was through Cowgate. As the name suggests, it was the route for the many herds of cattle being driven to Mauchline for the cattle fairs. In the main, the old thatched roof cottages in Cowgate have long since gone, including a single-storey cottage owned by Burns's father-in-law, James Armour. This cottage was situated on the west side of Cowgate, to the rear of the Whiteford Arms. From the back of the inn could be seen the garret window of the Armours' cottage and Burns and his future wife are reputed to have taken advantage of this situation to communicate with one another. When the cottage was demolished, the garret window was handed over to a local banker, William McMillan, and afterwards presented to the Burns Museum. Another of the four properties in Cowgate, once owned by James Armour, was badly damaged by fire in May 1909.

The present Mauchline Parish Church (pictured on the right from Cowgate around 1890) stands on the site of a much earlier church which was dedicated to St Michael and was one of the earliest known buildings in Mauchline. This earlier church was a smaller and plainer structure with a rudimentary wooden belfry. When the condition of the belfry deteriorated, the bell was removed and hung from a nearby tree, known locally as the Kirk End Tree. The church itself was demolished in 1827 and a new church opened on 2 August 1829. Designed by a local architect, William Alexander, the parish church is perpendicular in style. Its principal feature is the decorative turreted tower, which incorporates a belfry and clock. Of particular note are four gargoyles sculpted by Mr Thom, who was also responsible for the statues of Tam O' Shanter and Souter Johnie in the Burns Museum at Alloway.

Dating from about 1700, Poosie Nansie's initially had no signage on the exposed gable wall. However, around 1880, the lettering 'The Jolly Beggars Howff' was painted on to the gable wall and thirty years later the words 'Poosie Nansie's Hostelry' were added. The inn is equally well known by both names, although it is as the Jolly Beggars Howff that it appeared in the Burns poem of the same name. In time, the thatched roof was slated, although initially it was only the lower half which was replaced. The adjoining whitewashed, single-storey structure (at one time Jamieson's sweet shop) now forms part of the inn.

Poosie Nansie's Inn, Mauchline.

Old Kitchen, Poosie Nansie's Inn, Mauchline.

The old kitchen immediately inside, and to the right of the main entrance, has altered in appearance over the years. One of the changes is the absence of the eight day grandfather clock to the left of the picture. This was made by a Mauchline watchmaker and friend of Burns, John Brown. Like so many of Burns's friends and contemporaries, Brown was immortalised in his poetry when he wrote in *The Court of Equity*, 'If e'er ye gang to Mauchline toon, Be sure to call on Clockie Broon'. In Burns's lifetime, Poosie Nansie's was a rather seedy establishment, used by beggars and tramps. It was run by George Gibson (referred to by Burns as 'black-bearded Geordie') and his wife Agnes. On several occasions the Gibsons got into trouble for keeping a disorderly establishment. Even their servants were known to fall foul of the law. One of them, Agnes Wilson, was made to 'ride the stang' – allegedly for promiscuous behaviour. This punishment involved being tied to a pole and paraded through the streets. The Gibson's daughter, Janet, was depicted as Racer Jess in *The Holy Fair*, on account of the speed with which she carried out errands.

Earl Grey Street is named after Charles Grey, 2nd Earl Grey, a Whig prime minister from 1830 to 1834 who was prominent in the passing of the 1832 Reform Act and the abolition of slavery. The street, which was formed at the same time as New Street, replaced Cowgate as the principal entrance to Mauchline from the south. Many of the older properties in this 1905 picture remain today, including the eighteenth century Black Bull Inn at No. 51. In 1909 cab and carriage hirers J. & T. Gibson, advertising under the slogans 'Careful drivers' and 'First class turnouts', announced they had removed to the Black Bull Inn where they could make available cabs, wagonettes, dog carts, gigs and pony traps. Once a 'posting establishment', the arched doorway that at one time gave access to the stables at the rear of the inn remains today, but now gives access to flats built above the inn. Although many of the older businesses, such as McNeil's (draper), Bingham's (fishmonger) and the Co-operative Society, are now gone, others like J.D. & S. McMillan's (solicitors) and the Commercial Bank of Scotland (now the Royal Bank of Scotland) remain.

In this 1895 view of Cumnock Road, looking towards Mauchline, can be seen the servants of Viewfield and, beyond, a milkman with his horse drawn cart. Throughout the nineteenth century, Viewfield and the nearby church manse were the only properties on this stretch of road, but gradually other large villas were built. Some of these eventually catered for summer visitors, offering bed and breakfast accommodation. Viewfield, which is one of the most distinctive of these villas, was formerly the home of the Rev. Dr Patrick Wodrow. To left of the picture a road (later Station Road) led to the Haugh and to Ballochmyle Quarries. Just out of picture is the war memorial, which is situated at the junction of the Catrine Road and the Cumnock Road. This memorial was unveiled on 20 May 1927 by Sir Hugh Trenchard, Marshall of the Royal Air Force.

The red sandstone found around Mauchline has been mined since the eighteenth century and was once used extensively throughout Britain and even shipped to America. The two principal local quarries were Barskimming and Ballochmyle. The former was situated on the Ayr Road, near Mauchline Cemetery. It was established in 1891 by the Glasgow quarriers, Baird & Stevenson. Ballochmyle Quarry was situated off the Haugh Road and was operated by W. Gibson, an Auchinleck builder, until it was taken over by Marcus Bain in 1909. It remained in operation until the early 1950s. However, the demise of the industry had started around 1920, when brick began to largely replace the more expensive sandstone, so that today no quarrying is carried out locally.

The Haugh, once famously described by a local worthy as simply 'a collection of hooses', was in fact formerly the scene of Mauchline's early industry. It comprised a lint mill (later the Ballochmyle Creamery), a woollen mill and an ice stone factory. The woollen mill (the tall building to right of picture) burnt down in the mid-1920s, but the manager's house on Dam Road is still standing. The cottages alongside on New Road (including those on Old Row) were occupied by mill employees and later by families employed in the creamery. The ice stone (or curling stone) industry began at the Haugh. The original factory now forms part of Haugh Mill Farm, seen to the left of the picture.

Lacking basic facilities, such as bathrooms and a proper water supply, the cottages on New Row were eventually condemned and demolished in the late 1930s, with the families being rehoused in Mauchline. However, the owners of nearby Haughholm Farm (alongside the suspension bridge) were not deterred by the lack of such amenities, and remained where they were. The last occupant was Miss Marion (or Maisie) Inglis who died in 1964 at the age of ninety-one. Maisie, who lived on her own for the last nine years of her life, managed to survive without a supply of water or electricity! She also, apparently, had never been on a bus or gone to the cinema. Her sole pleasure was to listen to her battery-operated wireless!

Although usually the River Ayr is easily forded at the Haugh, when it is in spate the only means of crossing is by the bridge at Haughholm Farm. The bridge seen here to the right of the photograph is the old suspension bridge. This was known locally as the 'walking bridge', because it was too narrow to take a horse and cart. The present bridge dates from 1967 and replaces an earlier one (a successor to the 'walking bridge') which was swept away in the 1966 floods. The River Ayr and surrounding countryside have been badly affected by severe flooding throughout history. In 1940 the local Home Guard were called out to rescue cattle that had been swept down river when fields were flooded. Many of the cattle were found in the vicinity of the Enterkine railway viaduct – remarkably alive! Severe flooding affected most of the south-west of Scotland in 1966, with a landslip outside Sanquhar derailing the Glasgow to London express train. This same flooding swept away the successor to the 'walking bridge' – and left a resident in nearby Catrine with two trout on his front lawn!

Ballochmyle Creamery was built on the site of an eighteenth century lint mill. Around 1910, while in the hands of the McCrone family, the creamery was extensively altered in appearance, giving it a distinctive Swiss style. Robert McCrone, as well as being a pioneer in the manufacture of margarine products, was also the father of the novelist Guy McCrone, author of *Wax Fruit* and other popular novels. For many years a bust of Guy and three other members of the family graced the beautifully kept lawn which surrounded the creamery. The creamery was taken over in the 1920s by the German firm, Jürgens. When margarine production ceased, the property was used by M. Wiseman & Co. for the production of spectacle frames, but has lain disused since the 1980s.

The Creamery produced both 'Blue Band' and 'Seafoam' margarine. With respect to the latter, the manufacturers claimed it was 'superior in every respect to any butter' and it seems to have been particularly good for baking. The finished product, described as a 'butter substitute', not only benefited from a plentiful local supply of milk, but also from exceptionally clean water from a nearby artesian well. This, the manufacturers asserted, resulted in a 'sweet, clean, buttery' taste, making it a match for any similar product.

The road from Ballochmyle to Catrine. The latter village lies on the River Ayr, approximately two miles east of Mauchline. It was one of the destinations on the once popular twice-weekly coaching tours around Burns country. Visitors on the tour would catch the early morning train from Glasgow, arriving at Mauchline Station at 10.30 a.m. From there they would travel via Failford, Tarbolton and Mauchline itself, arriving at Catrine in time for lunch. After lunch they would visit Ochiltree, before returning to Mauchline in time to catch the 5 p.m. train for Glasgow. While in Catrine visitors were given the opportunity to visit the giant waterwheels of the Catrine cotton works. These works were established in 1787 by Claud Alexander of Ballochmyle in partnership with the philanthropist, David Dale. The wheels, each fifty feet in diameter, were constructed by Fairbairn & Willie of Manchester. When built, they were the largest in Scotland and were capable of handling 210 tons of water a minute.

Overlooking Gaans Holm, the Fog House (or Heather House), was situated within the Ballochmyle estate. It was erected by the nephew of Miss Wilhelmina Alexander (sister of Claud Alexander of Ballochmyle) to commemorate her meeting with Robert Burns in July 1786. Seemingly she met the poet one day while he was walking through the estate. Much taken by Wilhelmina, he afterwards composed, in her honour, the poem *The Lass o' Ballochmyle* and sent her a copy. It is said, however, that many years passed before Wilhelmina would acknowledge that she was indeed the 'lass'! The Fog House was constructed of twigs, moss and heather. It was nine feet wide and octagonal in shape, initially being open on three sides (eventually, as shown in this photograph, two of these sides were filled in). The remaining sides were panelled and inscribed either with symbols such as hearts and cupid's arrows or with verses of *The Lass o' Ballochmyle*. Unfortunately, having survived for many years, the Fog House was burnt down by vandals in 1944. Although there was talk of building a replica, the structure was never replaced.

The estate of Ballochmyle passed from the monks of Melrose to the Reids of Ballochmyle at the beginning of the seventeenth century. Around 1750 the estate was acquired by Sir John Whitefoord, a friend of Robert Burns and fellow mason. By 1786, however, having lost a considerable sum of money due to the collapse of a business venture, Whitefoord sold the estate to Claud Alexander, a partner in the Catrine cotton works. The house itself dates from around 1760 and was built in the Palladium style by John or Robert Adam. Between 1886 and 1890 a descendant, Sir Claud Alexander (the then owner) commissioned the architect Hew Montgomerie Wardrop to extend the house by adding a Victorian style frontage. In the 1940s the house was taken over and an Emergency Medical Services Hospital (one of seven in Scotland) was built alongside it, the house being used to accommodate medical and nursing staff. Initially, the hospital was used to treat servicemen wounded during the Second World War. As it specialised in the treatment of burns, it also tended to victims of the Clydebank Blitz. Latterly a general hospital, it is now closed and the house lies in ruins.